THE GAME: ten

The Game: tennis poems

WILLIAM SCAMMELL

PETERLOO POETS

First published in 1992
by Peterloo Poets
2 Kelly Gardens, Calstock, Cornwall PL18 9SA, U.K.

**A catalogue record for this book is available
from the British Library**

ISBN 1-871471-27 3

Printed in Great Britain by
Latimer Trend & Company Ltd, Plymouth

ACKNOWLEDGEMENTS: Some of these poems first appeared in *Bête Noire, Poetry Matters,* and *The London Magazine.*

'Golden Dawn' was published in *The Oxford Anthology of Sporting Literature* edited by Vernon Scannell (OUP, 1987)

PHOTOGRAPHS:

Front cover, page 10 and page 15: by courtesy of the Wimbledon Lawn Tennis Museum, from the book *Suzanne Lenglen— Tennis Idol of the Twenties* by Alan Little.

Page 33: by courtesy of Michael Cole Camerawork.

Back cover, and pages 10, 13, 19, 20, 21, 22, 23, 25, 37, 45: by courtesy of The Hulton Picture Company.

Contents

ARMS AND THE COURT

Summer pavilions. The cream of the cream
has trickled along to club and court,
lately risen from Lascaux's dream
to the art of geometric thought.

Who is this warrior, in snowy cloth
to freeze his intentions? What ancient race
is pending here, and who is the moth
of a girl who flutters all over the place?

The lyre has crumbled; the lyre's re-strung.
The grass glows like Achilles' shield.
Leaping down off the vase, they've flung
sheer carelessness at the weight of the world.

It's May, or it's June, when the greenery grows
long gawky limbs, and the cars go mad,
everything reeks, there's nothing to lose
but what was lost when the world was made.

They pause for a rest. Unscrewing the flask
they're lounging by the Lydian spring,
unbuttoned, still chasing after a wish
                and a brown arm flashing.

SUZANNE LENGLEN

There is one dress and one dress only
that Mlle Lenglen holds the patent of,
skill, beauty, power, La France in lonely
exaltation . . . six-love, six-love.

Imagine a princess, multiply by ten.
Imagine Anna Pavlova at her peak.
Imagine *the* most implacable swan
with a tennis racquet for a beak.

God help the Republic, God help Helen
Wills Moody, Gatsby, the masseuse
if Suzanne should miss a point, or ever loose

the bolt of her most telling
weapon, tears, whose soft *J'Accuse*
quells all the linesmen, up to heavenly Zeus.

Suzanne Lenglen
© *The Wimbledon Lawn Tennis Museum.*

10

BALL CHANGE: ANTECEDENTS AND PSYCHODRAMA

Real tennis was royal tennis,
kings and princes hazarding their arm.
(Who else could command a court?)

(*v*1515 to pay amorous attention to.)
(*sb*OE a clear space enclosed by walls.)
See *Conversations with Drummond*

for my Lord Northumberland's
classic early grump at a 'loss':
'I have played your worth'.

'Ye know not the worth
of a gentleman.' Frown, glare, stamp, scowl,
etcetera. The gentlemanly stuff

got off to an early start, thus
paving the way for tourneys
at Wimbledon and Forest Hills. Mad

self-expression got in early too.
See Ezroar *vs* Forty Mad-Dogs Whoofer
in Kensington Gardens, *circa* 1909, Ez

'sitting composedly in his square
and jumping up in time to receive
his adversary's ball . . . the flaps

of his polychromatic shirt flying out
like the petals of a flower. They just
went on till one or the other cried

"Game", "Hard luck", "My set"
or "Six sets to one". It was beyond
anyone to umpire or score.' Fordie

said it was like playing against
an inebriated kangaroo.
(Cf. Cochet, the Bounding Basque.)

Patrician certainly, bad-tempered
probably, not-quite-parfit knights
of the woeful dust, bashing a ball

with the gut of a cat; individualists
to a man. 'Whassamatter Drob?'
sang Emmo, paraphrasing the *Cantos*

as the shower stoutly
applauded his shining ass.
'Did you play like a cunt?'

THE PASSIONATE CLUBMAN
TO HIS LOVE

Come live with me, and mend my nerve.
You to *receive*, and me to *serve*.
Singly, *doubly*, we shall *play*
sweet *rallies*, all the livelong day.

Let others toy with Rocket, Roche,
spend Ivan's money, Gabby's looks.
Maria! come and be my coach
and we'll rewrite the history books!

Maria Bueno (Wimbledon 1964)
© *The Hulton Picture Company*

WILLIAM TATEN TILDEN II

The greatest ever, they say, in all
the top-ten lists compiled between
breakfast and the going down of the sun.

It was the Age of Brylcreem,
white flannels, biplanes,
short skirts and shingles, diamonds
as big as the Ritz;
and, waiting in the wings,
the impeccable Baron Gottfried von Cramm,
him with the fancy passing shots.

*

Now Boom-Boom Boris seizes Big Bill's throne,
winds up his serve, lays siege to Wimbledon
and takes it with a war-dance. Now and then
it falls to one of these gentle-giant men
to replay World War One, or Two, and stash
the enemies' foreskins up like so much trash.
Let Connors tremble . . .
                —What, that rabble-rouser,
all gamesmanship, and grunt, and mouth-and-trouser?
— Ees mucho macho, Señor, thees game, no?

— Yep, all the good things. Murder, sex, war. Slow
attrition, quick wits, nerve and sinew, Go-
go dancing, sunny billiards, mc squared,
Marvell acquitted, Milton running scared,
the Serpent for an umpire, Lewis Carroll
bodice-ripping in the Semi-Final . . .

— You joke, Señor! You deconstruct! You cannot be serious!
Ees time for you to sleep, to dream of Hana, grow delirious!

Big Bill Tilden with Suzanne Lenglen (July 1921)
© *The Wimbledon Lawn Tennis Museum*

BLASTED WITH CHAT

For Godsake hold your tongue, and let me watch,
    Or do your knitting, or the pools,
Ring up the weatherman, wind up your wools,
    Let out your chastity belt another notch,
        Go see your Mother, save your Son
        From that fool musique he's O.D.ing on
(I'd rather hear your Elton John),
    Look up your stars, write to Ed Koch,
    So you will let me watch.

Look, Ginny's got that Dutch girl on the ropes.
    She's even pounding to the net!
That backhand slice approach will come good yet
    For on it rides a kingdom's hopes
        Deferred these many summers, as
        The foreplay stalls, and our applause
Dies yet another death (it always was
        A heart in mouth affair). But cripes,
    Break out the bubbly, grab that monster punnet,
    Kiss me, Hardy! She's been and gone and done it!

THREE SETS LONG BY TWO SETS WIDE

In one of those sweet games I play'd
  where I could do no wrong.
The ball sang sweeter than a Maid
  who trips to Evensong.

Bereft of motion, lacking force,
  the other Finalist
knew Hope and Reason must divorce
  like Ramblers in a mist.

The day stood still. The joyful crowd
  applauded as I held the cup.
O mercy! to myself I cried
  if I should now wake up!

TIMOR MORTIS

Be near me when my game is poor
and all my passing shots are weak
and my opponent's six foot four
and clearly on a lucky streak.

Be near me when the balls don't bounce,
the sun shines straight into my eyes,
when all my smashes hit the fence,
my forehand just lies down and dies.

Be near me when the spiteful net
cord punishes my every clout.
Where were you when that cry of 'Let'
came hard upon that one of 'Out!'?

For god's sake, god, is this a hoax?
Where's the justice in that?
I might as well start making jokes
and juggling with my bat.

LEW HOAD

Pancho Gonzalez said that if earth
had to send just one player
to the Intergalactic Davis Cup
you'd be the one:
death in the afternoon
in the pitiless morse code of Wimbledon.

Follows a run of Sophoclean luck—
one more tiger with
a booze problem and a bad back.

Lew Hoad
© *The Hulton Picture Company*

EVONNE GOOLAGONG

'Beth fructuous, and that in litel space'
says Chaucer's pithy, ever-cheerful Host.
Too true. A smile broke out on Rosewall's face.

But most of all I'd bow to the finesse
of Little Mo, and V.J. Amrithraj,
and Evonne's easy, Abo, effortless

despatch. The rest could race.
The rest could bust their silly ass.
She was fructuous, in litel space

wrong-footing every expectation, Miss
Delightful 1972, Miss Nice,
soaring blissfully above the grass.

Evonne Goolagong (Ladies Final, Wimbledon 1972)
© *The Hulton Picture Company*

Bjorn Borg (Men's Singles Final Wimbledon 1979)
© *The Hulton Picture Company*

BJORN BORG

Eyes criminally close together,
fastest feet in the business,
Borg's groundstrokes would have landed
in Kensington but for one
small consideration: topspin.

He struck them as stepmothers
once brushed their daughters' hair.

Nobody knew what went on
behind that block of stone,
whether chess against a breaking wave
or just a corny Abba tune.

At the end of the end
he'd sink to his knees
in a parody of prayer
as the lightning went through him
eyes   fists   hair

A SATISFACTORY OUTCOME

Arthur's backhand was a menace
Jimmy couldn't read his play
Arthur went for Inner Tennis
It was always Arthur's day

Jimmy's grin was forced to grimace
Jimmy's grunt was blowing up
Arthur stuck to Inner Tennis
Arthur carried off the cup

Arthur Ashe (Albert Hall 1973)
© *The Hulton Picture Company*

Hana Mandlikova (Wimbledon 1981)
© *The Hulton Picture Company*

HANA MANDLIKOVA

'All icing', Ginny mused, 'but where's the cake?'
Rich, coming from a stale old currant bun.
God grant some English player half a stroke
from Hana's repertoire—e.g. a topspun

backhand, dropshot, chip, full-blooded drive;
a serve that's deep, and fast, and kicks, and's in;
a pair of legs that makes you glad to be alive;
passions you could light up a small country on.

23

JOHN McENROE

All Britain's deepest fears about spoilt brats
were thrillingly confirmed. You were THE PITS
John, an expression new to us. We heard
it as a ripe four-letter word
you'd dropped, splat! on the hallowed umpire's head.
At Wimbledon! Oh boy, but you were bad!
The nation's right arm ached, was overcome
with transcendental lust to smack your bum.
And Irish, too ... That baked-potato face,
that fallen-cherub frizz, that verbal mace
you sprayed at linesmen, paparazzi, anyone who'd got the gall to get their act between
your eye, the ball, your will, the clean
unanswerable line of pure perfection.

Stuffed shirts, stuffed balls, stuffed amateurs,
stuffed Royal Box, stuffed Chelsea Pensioners,
stuffed accents—*Pleeeaay!*—stuffed calls, stuffed sniggers, stuff
they know to handle Brooklyn way. Hang tough.

John McEnroe (Wimbledon 1985)
© *The Hulton Picture Company*

JUNIOR COACHING

Throw the ball up. Try to whack it
   over the net and in that square.
No no, Fiona! With the racquet!
   Tom, stop pulling Janet's hair.
Yes, Dave, racquets cost a packet.
   Oh, your dad's a millionaire.

That's all right then. What's his swindle?
   No, Tom, you can't smash just yet.
When you're tall and tough as Lendl . . .
   Darren, don't let down that net!
Now girls, who said you could spend all
   afternoon tormenting Brett?

Watch the ball! Turn! Arm back early!
   Bend your knees, and follow through!
Just like this. Look. Oh, well nearly.
   Now let's see what you can do.
Well done, Kimberley! You've clearly
   volleyed that to Timbuctoo!

Dave, I think your track suit's smashing.
   Yes, I like the headband too.
You've got the gear, you've got the passion,
   just like teenage McEnroe.
Now hit the ball, and try to ration
   all the things your mouth can do.

Pick up balls, please! Come on, quickly!
   Balls to me! Now who threw that?
Kimberley, you look quite sickly.
   What? You've lost your new school hat?
Thank you, Darren. Yes, it's triff'ckly
   tightly strung, your Becker bat.

Quiet! QUIET! Thanks a million.
    Got *all* your stuff? See you next week.
Kate, you may. In the pavilion.
    Well, there goes the nation's freak-
y, cheeky, whacky, billion brill ones
    piping homeward, in the peak!

SW19

The road is wide, the road is straight,
pilgrims queue at every gate,
camp out for fun.
Plush limos are put out to graze,
June's forehead wears a lovely blaze
at Wimbledon.

Fresh bunting waves, striped tents are up,
the bodies twirl, the blazers strut,
bronzed heroes run
with precious chains and high-bred rage
from love to deuce to middle-age
at Wimbledon.

Such arms, such legs! They brim with health,
terrestrial bliss, unearthly wealth,
stained gold by sun:
Renaissance men and women, born
to stamp their profiles on the lawn
at Wimbledon.

The umpire, stepped from heaven to earth,
gives rise to ribaldry and mirth:
his martyrdom
is sealed by groundlings' fickle calls
and foul abuse of bat and balls
at Wimbledon.

All England's here, from top to toe.
The air is like a radio
you twiddle on
from awps and erks and trendy jerks
to timeless medieval berks
at Wimbledon.

For hot dogs (cold) you queue and queue;
the strawbs are forced, and pale, and few;
the beer's a con;
but Members, high above it all,
are in the very deepest thrall
to Wimbledon.

They've castled K, unluckied Jim,
crossed beef with bile, laced cash with gin;
their colophon
is Kipling (*gules*) upon a ground
of patriotic racquets, found
at Wimbledon.

Still the ivy waves, and draws
in us spontaneous applause—
it feeds upon
a sacred grove of indrawn breath
where players play at sudden death
called Wimbledon.

HALL OF FAME

When it rains it all gets tricky.
The courts get wet, and the wicket sticky.
The TV boys have to do their stuff
ad lib in the studio. And things can get rough.

I remember the day when Desmond Lynam
spoke to a string of the past greats, when he could find them.
Hoad, Rosewall, Newcombe, they all stopped by
out of the wet and into the dry.

Des must've thought he'd struck pure gold
and, truth to tell, they looked not too old.
But talk? Evaluate? Comment? No way!
It is just not the good old Aussie way.

'What do you think of the modern game?'
'All right'. 'And these youngsters who shoot to fame?'
'All right'. 'And what about Mecir?'
'Not bad'. 'And Steffi?' 'Pretty fair'.

Even Desmond the Cool was a little nonplussed
to find his distinguished visitors so unfussed.
When Kenny came out with five words in a row
it lit up the entire studio.

So think not the commentator's job
is just a matter of knowing the ace from the lob.
No! There's far more than meets the eye
to this TV business. And by the bye

you've always to wear those little earpieces
whereby instruction from the producer never ceases,
to watch the clock and the autocue,
be right on the ball, and never never without a clue.

So here's a toast to Dan and his men
who've been to us all these years a good friend
in the matter of comments subtle and sage.
Long may they reign in this New Elizabethan Age!

beaming out from the Post Office Tower
the pomp and the pageant, even when there's a shower.
Yonder lies fame and fortune, I ween,
in the world-famous pastures of SW19!

EXTRA! EXTRA!
(The 1989 Finals)

Boris stands with arm round Steffi
smiling like a tickled chub.
Each holds up the winning trophy
      one and only winning trophy
at this year's All England Club.

Golden girl and boy of tennis!
Haloed youth's lopsided grin!
Here's Diana, here's Apollo
      shouting *follow follow follow*
down the coverts of the skin.

They say it's lonely on the mountain
desert islands are a bore.
I wish you more than fame and fortune
      that you learn to sing out your tune
on and off the tennis tour.

Bodies thrust their instincts at you
batting flesh around the court.
Minds are wild cards, stuck *in situ*
      (Me to serve? Why then, I'll fit you)
won't be moved, and can't be caught.

Steffi, keep on skating. Boris,
don't foresake that crosscourt drive.
I'll be Antiphon and Chorus
      sing my pennyworth of Chorus
just as long as you're alive.

Steffi Graf and Boris Becker (Wimbledon 1989)
© *Michael Cole Camerawork*

ROCK 'N ROLL TENNIS

It's no go the Aertex shirt, it's no go Fred Perry,
All we want is a sponsor, and a bucketful of the readies.
Their courts were made of mud and grass, with racquets stiff and
wooden,
And when the national anthem played they all stood to attention.

Jack Kramer, Jack the Lad, went pro, and took off with his circus,
Slugging out the best of five with speedy old Gonzalez,
Pittsburgh, Philly, Albuquerque, they jumped through rings of fire
For a couple of thousand lousy bucks on a Barnum & Bailey tour.

It's no go your Grace and Fry, it's no go Jesse Owens,
All we want is a pile upfront and a bimbo on the sideline.

Kenny Rosewall practised hard, threw a backhand volley
Deadlier than Cassius Clay, or Sally of our Alley,
Gathered all his trophies in, raced off with Drob and Lew
To play the best of ninety sets for peanuts in Kalamazoo.

It's no go your role models, strong and clean of jaw,
It's no go the wets and wimps of *Chariots of Fire*,
It's no go the *Boy's Own* stuff and those Olympic capers,
All we want is a video game and a pair of dayglo knickers.

Illy Nastase, Jimmy Connors, Mack the Knife, and me,
We took the rules and dunked them in the market economy,
Now grunts and groans will break the bones of every last opponent,
And of all the hotshots in the game, I am the heir apparent.

It's no go the playing fields and *Floreat Etona*,
It's no go the genteel lob, the tactical baseliner,
It's no go the mannerly Swede, no go Mr Nice Guy,
All we want is a Rambo stunt and the IQ of a frisbee.

POST-SCRIPT

It's gone to rack and ruin, chaps, it's all the way downhill.
We knock their brains out when we serve, we really play for real—
Just like Pancho, Newk and Sedgeman, just like ol' Suzanne
Batting the hell out of every ball, then curtseying to the queen.

And it's no go the wrinklies bit, the hands held up in horror,
The 'Game's gone all to pot!' brigade, the inveterate deplorer
Who gilds the past, and swipes the present from his rheumy face.
In another year you'll prop up the bar and say we were rather nice.

So you-know-what to your pastorals, your Chloris and Pomona.
We're into rock 'n roll, old boy, we shimmy to Madonna.
Just watch my ass. And tell me, pops, tell me loud and true,
Did anyone ever play better than us? The golden age is NOW!.

GOLDEN DAWN

A backhand slice is but a paltry shot,
no backbone in it, *sauve qui peut*, unless
hit to the corner baseline, asymptote
plus foxy coda, underspun duress
allowing one to charge in, tête-à-tête,
and do a hotshot number at the net.

When I was young and skinny, I'd not weight
enough to terrorise the baldest ball.
Now that I'm thick, and wise, and forty-eight
and compact of the waist chimerical
the drop-shot wounds me, and the high lob pains.
Either the body's lacking, or the brains,

it's never damn well right. And that's a shame.
O sages in your manuals, Kenny, Fred,
come be the singing-masters of my game,
that ace-tormented serve, weak overhead!
Iron out my faults. Let these joints thrive
and put some bottle in my cross-court drive!

Once in the rankings I shall never smoke
or swear, raise hell at discos, quarrel, swank.
If I can have a swimming pool, and poke
my troubles in the eye, break the odd bank,
I'll bow out gracefully, by fame paroled,
and sit up in the stands as good as gold.

Ken Rosewall (1970)
© *The Hulton Picture Company*

SENIOR COACHING

Today we have eye on the ball. Yesterday
we had keeping a good length. And tomorrow morning
we shall have following through. But today,
today we have eye on the ball. Monica's walking
backwards up the slide, down in the kiddies' playground,
  and today we have eye on the ball.

This is the sweet spot, greatly enlarged since
the old days. And this is your tapered beam,
which, without getting too technical, allows for greater
velocity through the air. Sweetness and light,
you might say—and never mind that screaming—
  for swatting the ball through the air.

This is a perfectly ordinary leather grip. No one
has ever improved on a leather grip, so please do not
let me see anyone turning up with one of those plastic
or composition jobs. You can hold it quite perfect if you
shake hands with your racquet. Darren's tumbling off the swing,
  and today we shake hands with our grip.

And this you can see is the preferred string tension
for maximum control of the ball, neither tight like Borg
nor droopy as Drobny. We call this cutting the crap
or everyman's option. It was developed by NASA during
the Swedish Campaign. There goes dad to the kiddies,
  hoping for instant control.

They call it everyman's option. It's up to you
how you treat your equipment, but I would advise you
to shake hands with the biggest sweet spot you can find,
hang on to your tapered beam, and keep following through,
for there are losses down in the playground
  and today we have eye on the ball.

THE TENNIS COURT OATH

I solemnly swear that I shall buy, regardless of cost, the biggest and best and latest break-through in tennis racquet technology not less than four months after its manufacture and launch, in the sure and certain hope that some of its magic will rub off on me, including Chrissie's groundstrokes and Stefan's first volley.

I hereby give assurance that I shall also splash out on the latest in leisurewear, no matter how tasteless the innovative riot of colour on my shirt, the track-suit billowing on my back, the winged contraptions on my feet.

I promise further that I will take out a small mortgage in order to buy new tennis balls, and undertake to turn a blind eye to this annual extortion practised on myself and other members of the British public.

I will endure bad courts, bad weather, amateur coaching, postal tournaments, LTA officials, saturation coverage of Wimbledon and no-TV-tennis-for-the-rest-of-the-year, home counties folie de grandeur, few or no indoor courts except school halls with multiple line-markings, tennis elbow, housemaid's knee, athlete's foot, hammer toes, callouses, tendonitis, server's torque, chronic abrasions of self-esteem, and promise not to complain, ever.

OUT OF THE PARK

There is tennis and there is lawn tennis,
the sea-borne heel springing like Aphrodite
from its shell of bone, erotomania for one
here at the all-England club of green.

And Marion's tennis dress
is pure Marion, which is to say
something short of a fit. She moves
like the two white cotton

bobbles at her heels,
her meticulous commentary
of shrieks and giggles
running parallel to the *actualité*.

*

A tree-coloured old man
is steering the white-liner over grass;
on the path a child pilots
his wobbly pushchair, which tacks

smartly down the camber till
we tumble over the cliff
of turf into mother's divided skirt.
Her dewy heels are tough. She fastens

the tilting buckle on her straps
and hoists the world to shoulder height
lisping syllables at the dark
round eye of the pedalling baby

set to stagger out of the park.

NOTES

'Arms and the Court' is a version of Osip Mandelstam's 'Tennis', poem no. 51 in *Stone* (1913), translated by Robert Tracy (Collins Harvill, 1991), p.147. Cf. *Ecclesiastes* IX, 10: 'Whatsoever thy hand findeth to do, do *it* with thy might, for *there is* no work, no device, no knowledge, nor wisdom, in the grave, whither thou goest'.

'Ball Change: Antecedents and Psychodrama'. Henry VIII, of course, is our most famous early enthusiast and promoter. I doubt that his courtiers were in much of a hurry to get down to Hampton Court to play him. Whether or not Sir Thomas Wyatt ever took him on—as he did, notoriously, in the amorous sphere— is open to scholarly question. Henry's dual interest in tennis and music reminds one that cat-gut was used to string both the racquet and the lute. Cf. *The Merchant of Venice*, V,i,83-88: 'The cat that hath no music in himself/Nor is not moved by concord of sweet sounds/Is fit for treasons, stratagems, and spoils . . . /Let no such cat be trusted'.

Lord Northumberland's classic piece of gamesmanship is recorded in Ben Jonson's conversations with his Scottish friend William Drummond in 1619. See *Ben Jonson: the Complete Poems* ed. George Parfitt (Penguin, 1975), p.473.

Ezra Pound versus Ford Madox Ford, *née* Hueffer (two of the big storytellers of all time), must have been a sight to behold. The beholders in this case were Brigit Patmore and Violet Hunt. See *A Serious Character: the Life of Ezra Pound* by Humphrey Carpenter (Faber, 1988), p.132.

Other notable literary tennis players of recent times include Vladimir Nabokov, Marianne Moore, Randall Jarrell, John Berryman (who I doubt could even see the ball, but competitiveness, in his case, stopped at nothing), and Alexander Solzhenitsyn, who allowed himself just one luxury, a tennis court, when he moved to Vermont and inherited his western royalties. Shakespeare obviously played billiards (see *Anthony and Cleopatra*,

II,v,3), a gentle first cousin of tennis, as did Tolstoy, Thackeray, Chekhov, and other clubbable men of letters. Russians and Americans seem to have a special fondness for tennis, which may have something to do with literary Anglophilia. (But see the opening page of Saul Bellow's *Dangling Man* for an alternative assessment of the Anglo-American sporting character.) Some writers, not all of them rotten, play cricket.

Emerson's tactful consolation of Drobny in the last verse is quoted verbatim from Gordon Forbes' *A Handful of Summers* (Simon & Schuster, 1978), one of the best tennis books ever written.

'The Passionate Clubman to his Love'. Verse two, line three: Bueno, of course, who was to my father what Pam was to Sir John Betjeman. Cf. Kipling's well-known 'If':

> If you can see a woman in full flower
> Lighting Centre Court up with her play
> And not be turned on by her grace and power
> You're certain daft, and should be put away.
>
> If you can meet with Chrissie, Steffi, Gabby
> Yet keep on reading Kierkegaard and Proust,
> Your morals and your id are pretty scabby.
> You'd better ask the chemist for a boost.
>
> If you can't get the flavour of it, laddy,
> There's them that will. They make the stars to run,
> Knowing it takes a goody and a baddy
> At fullest stretch to father any son.

'Three Sets Long by Two Sets Wide'. Thomas Love Peacock remarked that Shelley's Romantic melancholia, further inflamed by vegetarianism and free love, could be cured by eating three mutton chops, well peppered. Not even Peacock, however, had the temerity to think of applying this remedy to Wordsworth.

'Hall of Fame'. Whether or not William McGonagall, narrator of this well-deserved tribute, ever played tennis I have been unable to determine.

'Extra! Extra! (The 1989 Finals)'. For a glowing account of the nineteen-year-old Steffi in full flow at the US Open in 1989, the year in which she won the Grand Slam and the Olympic gold medal, see Garrison Keillor's *We Are Still Married* (Faber, 1990), pp.233-36. Boris's early fans have shown sign of disaffection with his behaviour in the last season or two. They misconstrue his impatience with himself. Only goody two-shoes and non-combatants think that losing is something you should do painlessly. Tain't in 'uman nature.

'Rock 'n Roll Tennis'. Verse two: see Jack Kramer's *The Game* (André Deutsch, 1981) for a graphic account of those memorable years. Kramer's egocentric, encyclopaedic knowledge of the game makes for an excellent read. (Ion Tiriac, the Romanian player-manager, looks set to become his modern equivalent, albeit a quieter model. Let's hope he writes a book too.)

Jack and Dan, incidentally, were the best commentatory duo the BBC ever put together, the Don Quixote and Sancho Panza of the airwaves.

Suzanne Lenglen (Wimbledon 1922)
© *The Hulton Picture Company*

PETERLOO POETS

'. . . a series kept up to scratch for a good few years by publisher Harry Chambers's energy and discrimination.'
Roy Fuller/Spectator

'Harry Chambers, the publisher of *Peterloo Poets*, continues to put to shame the London publishing houses, in the flow of attractively produced volumes coming from his press. The poet who finds his major outlet in the *Peterloo* series is fortunate indeed.'
D. M. Thomas/Arts South West·

'I share with others an admiration for the *Peterloo Poets* imprint, particularly the way they can put the fashionable to shame and produce winners from unlikely stables.'
Brian Jones/London Magazine

'*Peterloo Poets* is a small publishing house run by Harry Chambers in Cornwall. Its books are sensitively designed; each has a striking illustrated cover and the typography is excellent. The quality of production is much better than the usual standard of poetry paperbacks issued by major publishers.'
G. B. H. Wightman/British Book News

'There's a solid consistency about the *Peterloo Poets* series . . . Design and printing are always excellent, and the poems themselves are never less than interesting, not least because they tend to be by people who've already done some living and have something to say.'
Grevel Lindop/Times Literary Supplement

PETERLOO POETS

2 Kelly Gardens · Calstock · Cornwall PL18 9SA · UK